Measure It with Math!

MEASURING SPEED

Anne O'Daly

PowerKiDS press

Published in 2024 by The Rosen Publishing Group, Inc.
2544 Clinton Street, Buffalo, NY 14224

Portions of this work were originally authored by Chris Woodford and published as *Speed.*
All new material this edition authored by Anne O'Daly.

Children's Publisher: Anne O'Daly
Design Manager: Keith Davis
Picture Manager: Sophie Mortimer

Picture credits:

Key: t = top, tr = top right, b = bottom

Front Cover: 123RF: tr; Shutterstock: Constantin Losif l, Eugene Onischenko tl, Scanrail1 r.
Interior: Halfpoint 5, tomazi 18; NASA: USAF 22; Shutterstock: Atstock Productions 4, Anton Balazh 15, Martin Bergsma 12, Jaromir Chalabala 25, Supa Chan 26, CP DC Press 10–11, daniiD 19, FotoRequest 23, Janossy Gergely 7, Peter Jurik 24, Knumina Studios 17, Mega Pixel 28l, Nalidsa 6, Alexey Nikitin1981 14, W. Photanan 27, Patrick Poendi 13, Rawpixel.com 29t, Mauro Rodrigues 20, E.V. Safronov 1, 8, slowmotiongi 16, Vlad333 6.

Cataloging-in-Publication Data

Names: O'Daly, Anne.
Title: Measuring speed / Anne O'Daly.
Description: New York : Powerkids Press, 2024. | Series: Measure it with math! | Includes glossary and index.
Identifiers: ISBN 9781642827828 (pbk.) | ISBN 9781642827835 (library bound) | ISBN 9781642827842 (ebook)
Subjects: LCSH: Speed--Measurement--Juvenile literature.
Classification: LCC QC137.52 O34 2024 | DDC 531'.112--dc23

Manufactured in the United States of America

CPSIA Compliance Information: Batch #CSPK24. For further information contact Rosen Publishing at 1-800-237-9932.

Contents

What Is Speed?

A jet plane zooms through the sky. A snail creeps along the ground. Both are moving, but the plane moves quickly and the snail moves slowly. Whether they are fast or slow, all moving objects have speed. Speed is a measurement of how fast something is moving.

FACT

It takes ten times as long to drive from New York to Los Angeles as it does to fly between the cities.

Speed is also the time it takes to travel a set distance. Think about going from one end of a street to the other end. A car will get there more quickly than a person walking. The distance is the same, but the car's speed is faster than the person.

People run at different speeds. The winner of a race is usually the person who ran the fastest!

VELOCITY OR SPEED?

People often talk about speed and velocity. But what's the difference? Velocity measures the speed of something and its direction. Speed doesn't have a direction. Two cars can have the same speed. But if they are driving in opposite directions, they have different velocities. If a car changes direction, its velocity changes, even if the car stays at the same speed.

Units for Speed

Speed measures how fast something is moving. To figure out an object's speed, we need to know how far it traveled. And we need to know the time it took. Speed is the distance divided by the time:

Speed = distance ÷ time

If a car drives 30 miles in one hour, its speed is 30 miles per hour. Its speed is the distance traveled in an hour.

The space shuttle reached a speed of 1,000 miles per hour just a minute after it took off.

TRY THIS

HOW FAST DOES IT MOVE?

Can you work out the missing speeds? (Answers on page 32.) Remember:

Speed = distance ÷ time

A family car drives 55 miles in 1 hour.

How fast did it go?

An airplane flies 500 miles in 1 hour.

How fast has it flown?

A person walks 10 miles in 2 hours.

How many miles per hour is this?

A train travels 350 miles in 1 hour.

What was its speed?

Speeds of fast-moving objects like cars and trains are measured in miles per hour. Miles per hour are units of speed. A unit tells us how big a measurement is. We measure the speeds of slow objects in different units. A snail crawls along at about 30 inches per hour.

A sloth has a top speed of about 0.15 mile per hour (0.24 km/h).

Metric Speeds

To figure out speed, we need to know distance and time. In the United States, distance is measured in miles, feet, and inches. These are called imperial units. If imperial units are used to measure distance, the speed is also measured in imperial units. Imperial measurements of speed include miles per hour and feet per second.

Race cars can reach speeds of 223 miles per hour. That is the same as 360 kilometers per hour.

Metric Units

Most countries use metric units for distance. Metric units include kilometers (km) and meters (m). If distance is measured in metric units, the speed is also measured in metric units. Metric measurements of speed include meters per second and kilometers per hour.

FACT

1 mile per hour in imperial units is the same as 0.4 meter per second in metric.

TRY THIS

IMPERIAL TO METRIC

1 mile per hour (mph) is the same as 1.6 kilometers per hour (km/h)

We multiply the speed in mph by 1.6 to get the speed in km/h.

Question: If a car travels at 50 miles per hour, how fast is it going in kilometers per hour?

This road signs shows speeds in miles per hour (mph) and kilometers per hour (km/h).

METRIC TO IMPERIAL

1 kilometer per hour is the same as 0.6 mile per hour.

We divide the speed in km/h by 1.6 to get the speed in mph.

Question: If a plane travels at 2,000 kilometers per hour, how fast is it going in miles per hour?

Answers on page 32.

Fast and Faster

Olympic athletes are fast! So are race cars and jet planes. But their speed can still be measured. Whether things go fast or slow, their speed is always the distance divided by the time it takes.

Speed = distance ÷ time

This is always true, whether we use imperial or metric units.

We cannot tell how fast a runner is going just by looking. But we can time how long the runner takes to run 100 yards or 100 meters. That will tell us the runner's speed.

Jamaican athlete Usain Bolt (in the yellow shirt) holds the world record for the fastest ever 100-meter race.

TRY THIS

RUNNING AND DRIVING

If an athlete runs 1 mile in 6 minutes, what is his or her speed in miles per hour? (Clue: 6 minutes = 1⁄10 hour)

What is their speed in kilometers per hour?

(Don't forget: 1 mile = 1.6 kilometers)

A person drives from New York to Boston. The distance is 200 miles, and the journey takes 4 hours. What is the average speed in miles per hour?

What is the speed in kilometers per hour?

Answers on page 32.

People and Machines

One way to measure the speed of a plane is to time how long it takes to fly a distance. It takes a plane about 5 hours to fly from New York City to Los Angeles.

The distance between the cities is about 2,400 miles. So the plane flies at a speed of 2,400 miles divided by 5 hours, or 480 mph.

FACT

In the world athletic championships in 2009, Usain Bolt ran 100 meters in 9.58 seconds.

Slow Growing

Some objects move so slowly that we don't notice it. Many things in nature happen slowly. Our hair and fingernails are growing all the time. Plants grow from a tiny seed. But most grow so slowly that we don't see it. It can take hundreds of years for a tree to grow.

FAST FORWARD

One way we can see very slow speeds is to speed them up. We could leave a camera running for a day or a week so it films a flower opening. Then we could speed up the movie to show the flower opening more quickly. This is called time-lapse photography. Many TV nature programs use it.

Nanga Parbat mountain in Pakistan is growing at a speed of 0.25 inch (0.6 cm) a year.

FACT

The Adirondack Mountains in the United States are growing by about 0.11 inch (3 mm) each year.

Slowest Speeds

Changes can happen even more slowly. Some mountains are growing higher by a very tiny amount every year. Earthquakes happen around cracks in the Earth called fault lines. Fault lines move about a quarter inch per year. Sometimes, this slow movement can lead to a huge earthquake, causing a lot of damage.

Spinning Around

Objects don't just move in a straight line. Some go around in a circle. Moving in a circle is called rotating, or revolving. Lots of things move like this.

A Ferris wheel at a carnival rotates. Speed is the distance traveled in a certain time. If something moves in a circle, it does not travel. But that does not mean its speed is zero. We need a different way to measure speed for something that rotates.

Spinning speeds can be fun! A carnival ride rotates about twice per minute.

ROTATING PLANETS

All the planets are constantly rotating around themselves and around the sun. It takes a year for Earth to make one journey around the sun. So Earth's speed is one rotation per year. Earth also spins as it moves around the sun. It takes one day for Earth to rotate once. So Earth's spinning speed is one rotation per day.

Earth spins in space as it moves around the sun.

FACT

The rotor blades of a helicopter spin around at 500 revolutions per minute.

Revolutions per Minute

Instead of distance, we measure how many times the object makes one complete turn. Each turn is called one rotation, or revolution. If a spinning top turns around 10 times in 1 minute, its speed is 10 revolutions per minute, or 10 rpm. When a washing machine spins clothes, it rotates at 1,000 rpm!

Speeding Up, Slowing Down

Things don't always travel at the same speed. They speed up and slow down. A race car starts a race at the starting line. Its speed is zero. The car speeds up until it reaches its top speed. At the end of the race, it slows down and stops. When something speeds up, this is called acceleration. When it slows down, it is called deceleration.

Acceleration tells us how fast something gets to its top speed. A race car accelerates quickly. It can go from 0 to its top speed in just a few seconds. A heavy truck accelerates slowly.

A cheetah can accelerate from 0 to 60 miles per hour (97 km/h) in just three seconds.

The parachute on this truck helps it slow down.

SPEEDING UP

Suppose a car is driving at 25 mph. The driver steps on the gas for 10 seconds and the car speeds up to 55 mph. We can measure the acceleration in the following way. First, we need to know how much the speed has changed. It is 55 mph minus 25 mph, or 30 mph. The change in speed took 10 seconds to happen. So the acceleration is 30 mph in 10 seconds.

Why Do We Measure Speed?

Measuring speed can keep us safe. Drivers have to know how fast they are going to stay safe and keep at or below the speed limit. An instrument called a speedometer measures the car's speed. It works by counting how quickly the car's wheels turn around. It turns this into speed.

PHOTO FINISH

Some races are very fast. It can be hard to tell who won. Most athletic tracks have a camera at the finish line. As the runners cross the line, the camera takes photos of them. The pictures show the winner and how fast they were running.

Photographs can show who was the fastest in a race.

TRY THIS

TIMING THE DISTANCE

We can tell how fast people or horses are going by timing how long they take to run a certain distance. If someone runs 100 yards in 15 seconds, his or her speed is 100 divided by 15, or 6.7 yards per second.

100 ÷ 15 = 6.7 yards per second

Now try these:

If an athlete runs 800 meters in 2 minutes and 40 seconds, how fast are they going?

If a horse runs 2 miles in 4 minutes, how fast is it running?

Answers on page 32.

Athletes and Speed

People measure speed during races. Races take place over a set distance. Some races are short—100 yards or 100 meters. A marathon is 26.2 miles (42 km). A sprinter is faster than a marathon runner.

A speedometer shows a car's speed in miles per hour and kilometers per hour.

Speed at Sea

Speed at sea has its own special unit called a knot. Sailors used to measure the speed of ships with a rope. The rope had knots along its length. Sailors dropped the rope off the back of the ship and counted the knots. The faster the ship was going, the faster the rope fell into the water. The ship's speed was measured in knots per hour.

A powerboat can speed over the waves at 100 miles per hour (160 km/h).

MAKING WAVES

Waves on the sea have their own speed. If a boat moves with the waves, the waves make it go faster (**1**). The boat's real speed is the speed of its engine plus the speed of the waves. If the boat moves against the waves (**2**), the waves slow it down.

1. Boat's speed = speed of engine + speed of waves

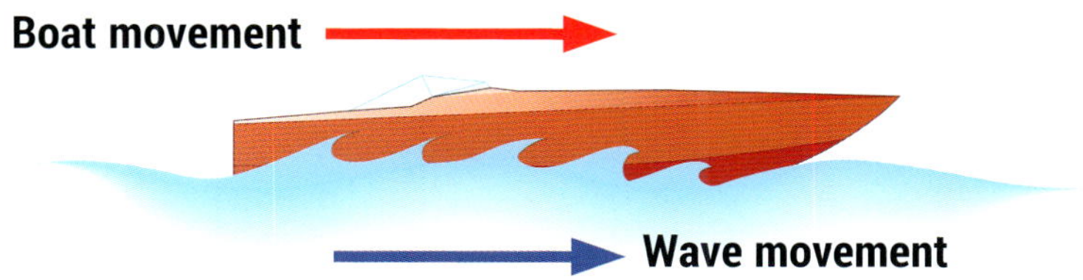

2. Boat's speed = speed of engine – speed of waves

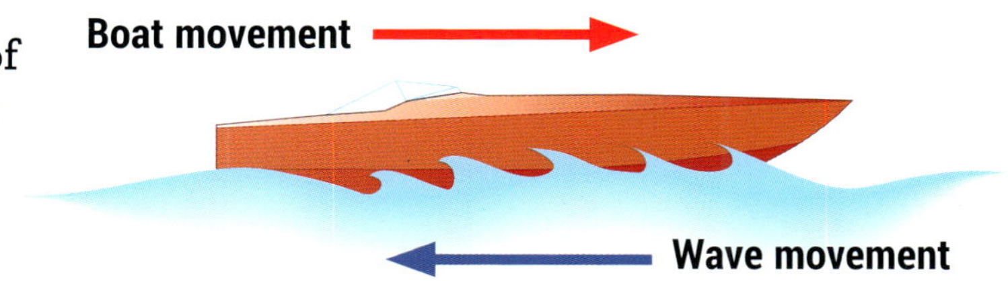

Modern Measurement

Modern ships have speedometers, like cars or airplanes. But their speed is still measured in knots. One knot is 1.1 mph (1.8 km/h). A ship that moves at a speed of 20 knots is going at 22 mph (35 km/h).

FACT

The fastest boat was called *Spirit of Australia*. It reached 317.6 miles per hour (511.1 km/h).

Fast Flyers

Have you ever watched an airplane fly overhead? Airplanes are the fastest things most people see. Passenger airplanes fly at between 500 and 700 miles per hour (800 and 1,100 km/h). But some planes are much faster.

Faster than Sound

Some planes fly faster than the speed of sound. Sound waves travel through air at about 760 mph (1,216 km/h) near the ground, or more slowly at higher altitudes. As planes fly at this speed, they make a loud noise called a sonic boom. It can be heard from the ground.

The Lockheed SR-71 Blackbird is the world's fastest aircraft. It can reach speeds of 2,100 mph (3,500 km/h).

TRY THIS

SPEED IN FLIGHT

Can you calculate the speed of these aircraft? Remember, speed is distance divided by time.

An airplane flies 75 miles in 15 minutes. **What is its speed?**

A supersonic plane flies 400 miles in 30 minutes. **What is its speed?**

A hypersonic rocket flies 1,000 miles in 10 minutes. **What is its speed?** What is the same rocket's speed in kilometers per hour? (1 mile = 1.6 kilometers.)

Answers on page 32.

FACT

Planes can fly faster when they are higher in the sky. The air is thinner and easier to fly through.

Supersonic

Planes that fly faster than the speed of sound are called supersonic. They have sleek noses and wings to cut through the air. Hypersonic rockets fly at least five times faster than sound, at about 3,300 miles per hour (5,300 km/h).

The fastest bird is the peregrine falcon. It flies high, then dives at up to 200 miles per hour (320 km/h) to catch its prey.

Space Speed

The universe is enormous. And it's getting bigger all the time. In 1929, U.S. astronomer Edwin Hubble wanted to find out how fast the universe was growing. He had to figure out how he could measure a speed like that.

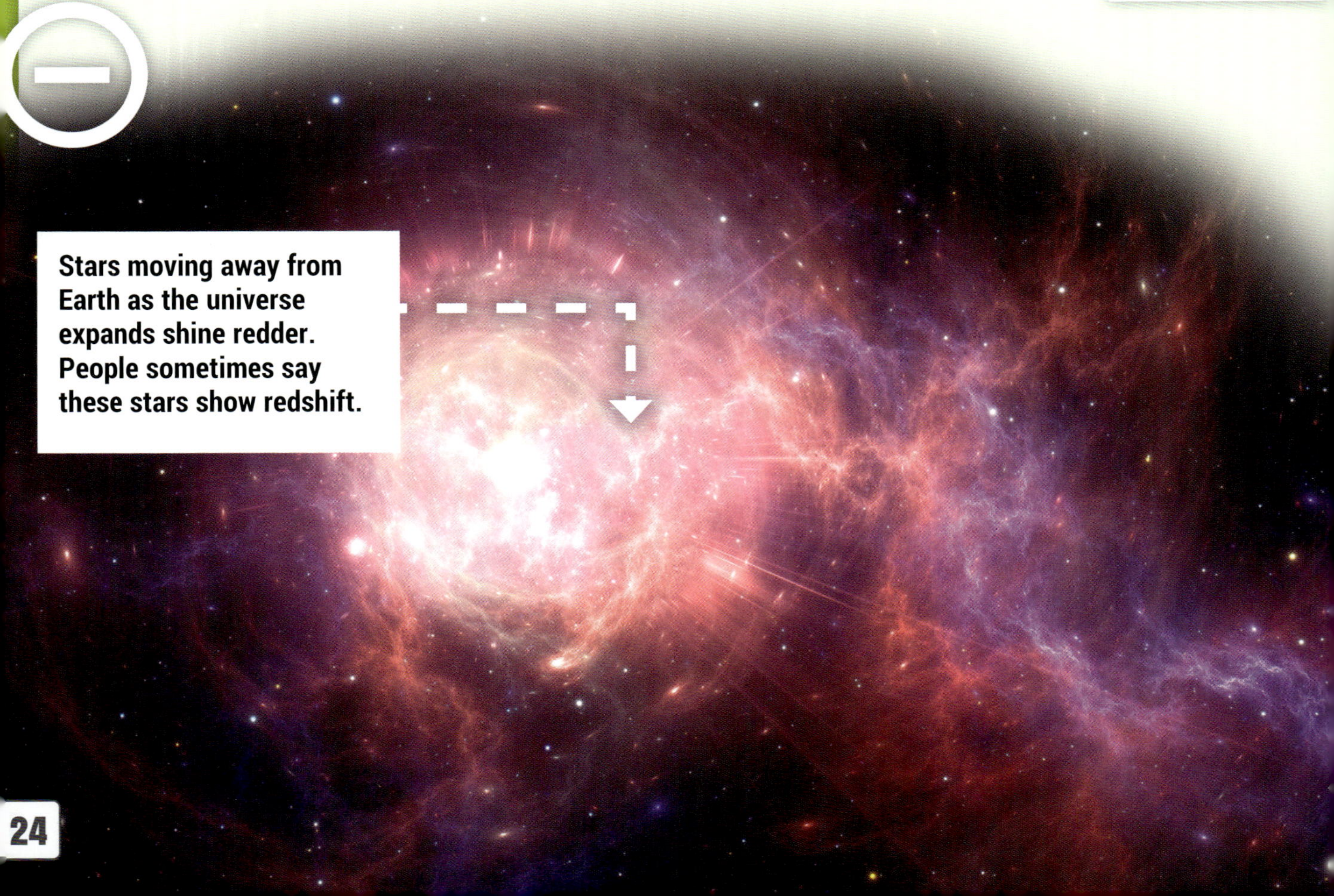

Stars moving away from Earth as the universe expands shine redder. People sometimes say these stars show redshift.

DOPPLER EFFECT

When a fire truck rushes past, its siren seems to get lower. That happens because the speed of the truck changes the way sound waves travel from the siren. When the truck comes toward you, its speed makes the siren sound higher. When the truck rushes past, the truck's speed makes the siren sound lower. The change is called the Doppler effect. And it also makes the redshift in starlight.

FACT

Light from a bright star called Sirius takes more than eight years to reach Earth.

Star Shine

As the universe gets bigger, stars move away from Earth. That changes the way we see their light. If stars are moving away, they seem to shine a little redder. That is called redshift. Hubble measured how fast stars are moving by measuring how red they looked. That told him how fast the universe is getting bigger.

Fastest of All

Light is the fastest thing in the universe. It travels at the incredible speed of 186,291 miles (298,066 km) per second. Nothing can go faster than that. It took scientists many years to measure the speed of light.

Galileo's Experiment

In the 17th century, a famous Italian scientist named Galileo Galilei (1564–1642) tried to measure the speed of light. He flashed a lantern to a friend some distance away. But he found light travels too fast to measure its speed like that.

FACT

It takes just over 8 seconds for the sun's rays to reach the surface of Earth.

DEAD STARS

Some of the stars we can see are no longer there. They stopped shining millions of years ago. But they are so far away that the light they sent out is still traveling toward Earth. If a light beam has to travel from one side of the universe to the other, it can still take millions of years for it to reach Earth.

Speed of Light

In the 1850s, a French scientist named Armand Fizeau (1819–1896) became the first person to measure the speed of light. He used a spinning wheel to make a light beam travel a very long way. He timed the light beam and that gave him a measurement for the speed of light.

Light Years

Distances in outer space are so great that people measure in light-years. A light-year is the distance a beam of light can travel in one year. It is the same as 5.9 trillion miles (9.5 trillion km).

HANDS ON

How Fast Are You?

WHAT YOU NEED

* Ruler or tape measure
* Stopwatch or watch with a second hand
* Some chalk
* Long, straight path
* A friend

WHAT YOU DO

This May Help

It is not easy to make accurate timings. If you use a stopwatch, make sure you start it at exactly the same moment as you say "Go!" If you are using an ordinary watch, get your friend to start walking or running just as the watch hand reaches 12.

1. Draw a line on the ground with the chalk. Measure a distance of 100 yards or 100 feet away. Make another mark on the ground at the end of the distance.

2. Walk from one chalk line to the other. Ask your friend to time you.

3. Figure out your speed by dividing the distance by the time.

4. Now run slowly between the chalk marks. Figure out your speed again. Try running more quickly. How much faster were you?

5. Change places with your friend and repeat the steps again.

Glossary

acceleration A change in speed that makes something go faster.

centimeter A small metric unit of measurement equal to one meter divided by 100.

deceleration A change in speed that makes something go slower.

Doppler effect The way speed changes the observed light or sound of a moving object.

hypersonic A speed that is at least five times faster than the speed of sound.

imperial A traditional measurement. Miles, feet, and inches are imperial units of measure.

kilometers per hour A metric measurement of speed. There are 1,000 meters in a kilometer.

km/h A short way of writing "kilometers per hour."

knot A measurement of speed at sea (1 knot equals 1.1 miles per hour).

measurement A way of finding out how tall, long, big, or fast something is.

meter A metric measurement equal to about 3.3 feet.

metric system A modern system of measurements based on the meter.

miles per hour An imperial measurement of speed.

mph A short way of writing "miles per hour."

motion Another way of describing movement.

redshift The way distant stars seem to be redder because they are moving away.

revolution One complete turn of a spinning object.

rotation One complete turn of a spinning object.

speedometer A gauge that measures speed in a car, truck, or bike.

supersonic A speed that is faster than the speed of sound.

unit The part of a measurement that tells us how big or small it is: inches, feet, and miles, for example.

velocity A speed measured in a certain direction.

Find Out More

BOOKS

Allan, John.
Mighty Mechanics' Guide to Speed: From Racing Cars to Roller Coasters.
BeetleBooks, 2022.

Askew, Mike.
Let's Measure It
(You Can Master Math!).
Rosen Publishing, 2022.

Owen, Ruth.
A Book of Speed Fiend Projects for Kids Who Love to Go Fast.
Rosen Publishing, 2022.

Vilardi, Deborah.
Amazing Feats of Speed.
Capstone Publishing, 2019.

WEBSITES

www.coolkidfacts.com/speed-and-velocity/
Fun introduction to speed and velocity, with illustrations, diagrams, and links.

www.ducksters.com/science/physics/speed_and_velocity.php
Information about speed and velocity.

www.mathsisfun.com/measure/speed-velocity.html
Speed and velocity explained, with examples and links.

tech25s.com/25-facts-about-speed-interesting-and-surprising-facts/
Twenty-five amazing facts about speed.

Publisher's note to educators and parents: Our editors have carefully reviewed these websites to ensure that they are suitable for students. Many websites change frequently, however, and we cannot guarantee that a site's future contents will continue to meet our high standards of quality and educational value. Be advised that students should be closely supervised whenever they access the Internet.

Index

ANSWERS

Page 7: car, 55 mph; airplane, 500 mph; person, 5 mph; train, 350 mph. **Page 9:** 80 km/h; 1,250 mph. **Page 11:** 10 mph/16 km/h; 50 mph/80 km/h. **Page 19:** 5 meters per second; 30 mph. **Page 23:** 300 mph; 800 mph; 6,000 mph, or 9,600 km/h.